OF GRUNGE AND GOVERNMENT

OF GRUNGE AND GOVERNMENT
LET'S FIX THIS BROKEN DEMOCRACY!

BY KRIST NOVOSELIC

RDV Books
New York

Published by RDV Books/Akashic Books
©2004 Krist Novoselic

Editorial Assistance: Gillian Gaar
                        Rob Ritchie
Cover Photographs: Patricia Ridenour

ISBN: 0-9719206-5-6
Library of Congress Control Number: 2004106232
Printed in Canada
First Printing

RDV Books/Akashic Books
PO Box 1456
New York, NY 10009
Akashic7@aol.com
www.akashicbooks.com

CONTENTS

Chapter 1: Music Must Change

SOCIETY OFFERS MANY LABELS for people who run against the grain. But it's the people on the so-called fringes who actually bring change. Without rebels, rabble-rousers, malcontents, or whatever label we choose to apply, the culture would remain static.

Look around the world at cultures that squash expression—their resistance to change has left them stuck in the 19th century. And while many in our nation disparage those who diverge from the status quo, it's people who made their own way that created the United States. Our founders refused a monarchy whose power was derived from heredity. The notion of a republic of the people, by the people, and for the people shattered the old paradigm. The new republic, the United States of America, acknowledged freedom as a basic tenet of human experience.

Independence in the U.S. guarantees individuals the right to speak. But independence must also speak to us.

It was in 1983 that I walked into a bookstore in Seattle's University District asking for anything by Jack Kerouac. The clerk, with a broad grin, walked over to a shelf and handed me *The Dharma Bums*. Reading Kerouac confirmed the sense of independence I have always felt. *The Dharma Bums* is about the journey of life and meaningful connection with people. The story culminates in the classic journey to the mountain, where the protagonist, Japhy, ends up in a fire lookout tower in Washington State. A Zen hermit experience is conveyed in quintessential beat prose; there, alone, he transcends time and self in an exploration of inner-space. Every moment is savored, every simple action a meaningful experience. It's as if he is living his last days on earth. In his subsequent work, Kerouac left the isolation of the mountain to return to society. His world was not confined to the tail-fins and poodle-skirts of 1950s popular culture. He lived in the subterranean realm of the beat generation. Subcultures are where many people who are not inclined to adhere to conformity connect with others of the same ilk. Independence is not isolation.

I grew up in Aberdeen, Washington in the early 1980s and had a lot of fun there. But eventually I began to grow away from the party crowd that made up my social life. In the mid-1960s, smoking marijuana was a political statement, the counterculture's answer to the mainstream martini crowd. But by the time it hit my scene, pot was a cliché icon, something fundamental to the identity of people referred to as "stoners." There is a certain comradery that manifests itself in the course of passing a joint around; unlike sharing a beer, the illegal act of smoking pot demonstrates actual humanity in the face of abstract prohibitions. But to many stoners, marijuana was more about escapism than real liberation. If anything, "drop out" was the only relevant term left of Timothy Leary's famous axiom, *"Turn on, tune in, drop out."* The stoner message was: "Don't expect anything from me." It was antiestablishment, and petty resistance was sometimes acted out in the world of traffic court, with stoners (like many others) subject to a seemingly endless cycle of DUI and wrong-turn tickets and fines paid on installment. Stoners were in a lower economic strata, locked in a punitive relationship with their government based on issues regarding the secondary task of transportation. It was token rebellion against the forces that threatened a Saturday night party. "Stoner" was a counterculture without a mission.

As far as the music of that scene went, the slick, canned sounds of mainstream heavy metal didn't appeal to me. In 1980, I lived in what was then Yugoslavia for a year. A lot of music came down from London; I heard punk rock and caught much of the ska scene of the time. Yugoslavia also had a homegrown scene with good, diverse music. But when I returned to the U.S., I found that it was hard for punk to make its way to Aberdeen because of its geographic isolation. Still, it trickled in the best it could. I watched *New Wave Theatre* on the U.S.A. Network or heard punk on Sunday night specialty shows on FM radio stations. Gradually, here and there, I picked up on a style of music I knew was controversial. It eventually gained a foothold, thanks to the efforts of some truly independent young minds.

I met Buzz Osborne and Matt Lukin while working after school in a fast-food restaurant. These fellows were in an actual punk band, the Melvins! And Buzz was not only up on the music, he also had an excellent grasp of the whole ethic of punk subculture. I needed a breath of fresh air and was immediately intrigued. These new sounds were raw and vital. I started buying the music emanating from underground scenes in San Francisco, Los Angeles, Washington, D.C., and other places. Punks were also connected through do-it-yourself (DIY) publishing. Fanzines were the blogs of the early '80s. Anything went with the zines; they not only covered music, there was a heavy dose of politics as well. Of course they were antiestablishment, and most were left-wing, promoting vegetarianism, drug-free living, and anticorporatism. They were truly independent and decentralized, in stark contrast to the mainstream media I was used to. They were part of an alternative economy promoting small, independent business. For me, punk wasn't a fad; it offered meaning in a society that didn't offer enough.

Punk rejected the mainstream—which was just as well, because the mainstream rejected punk. Safety pins through the nose, loud clothing, and spiked hair scared most people. Too many associated self-destructive violence with punk. Punk was supposed to annoy and antagonize society, and indeed it did. In the early '80s, punk rockers were despised and ridiculed by their peers in the stoner crowd; the spiked growl of punk upset the soft feathers of Camaro hairstyles. One time, while standing in front of a club with some friends, we got hit by eggs tossed out of a passing muscle car. Laughing, we wiped away the egg on our tattered flannel with the same hands we used to wash away society's conformity. Self-assured in our personal liberation, ridicule from conformists couldn't upset true punks.

I started shopping for clothes at the Salvation Army in an attempt to subvert consumerism (I had little money anyway). In 1983, cool clothing from the '50s and '60s really wasn't that old; this was right before the vintage/collectable industry started scooping things up. As a badge of my independence, I dressed differently from the status quo, and, unlike some punks, I didn't dress dangerously. I didn't have a mohawk or a studded leather jacket. I didn't throw away my Aerosmith or Led Zeppelin records either. I'd hear punks refuting the old guard—they cast '70s rock bands away as though they were false prophets; those who followed old-school rock ran the risk of being taunted by these self-appointed guardians of the new order. This was simply pop music turning through its cycle of reinvention, but with a big dose of ideology mixed in. Some fanzines were very dogmatic, demanding a purity of ethic. Even though I was a believer in punk, how could I reject the music that gave me so much joy? Where would the world be without Black Sabbath? If punk was about freedom, why conform to some kind of molded identity? If I wanted to wear a uniform, I'd join the military. I believe that punk is a state of mind. It's about making your own way. And regardless of orthodoxy, I felt punk was messianic. In a lot of ways it did save me. An alternative vision didn't have to be stuck in the hippy 1960s—it was reborn through punk! A new generation was offered the promise of liberation from the status quo. And we were given community to boot.

In 1984 I traveled with Buzz and Matt to Walla Walla, Washington to see Black Flag perform. We drove across the state in a 1968 VW van painted like a zebra. Black Flag was on a mission to bring punk to the hinterlands, going out of their way to play small towns off the beaten path. Lead singer Henry Rollins sang of alienation with lyrics like, "*Swimming in the mainstream/Is such a lame dream.*" Their music was slow and sludgy at that point, closer musically to Black Sabbath than the Sex Pistols. But it was also free of the boundaries of genre and era. It was real, and that's all that really mattered. There must have been a few dozen kids in the large community center that held the show. But as far as the mainstream media went, the tour wasn't swimming at all because, like the Sex Pistols, Black Flag was too dangerous.

The Melvins were looking for a new drummer, so I introduced Matt and Buzz to thundering teen drummer Dale Crover. They started practicing at Dale's house, and soon the Crovers's back porch and yard became a local hangout. American hardcore/punk was known for its blistering speed, but by '84 this was changing. Buzz started writing slow and heavy riffs. This dirge-like music was the genesis of Northwest Grunge.

This is around the time I met this person named Kurt Cobain. If I am to speak about independence, I need to mention one of the most independent people I've ever met. Kurt was a completely creative person—a true artist. He had just got a job and found his own place. What a den of art/insanity that was! He tried to make his own lava lamp out of wax and vegetable oil (it didn't work). He sketched very obscene *Scooby-Doo* cartoons all over his apartment building hallways (they were done very well). He made wild sound montages from obscure records. He sculpted clay into scary spirit people writhing in agony. He played guitar, sang, and wrote great tunes that were kind of off-kilter. Punk, pop, or whatever, it was raw creativity. Kurt held a skeptical perspective toward the world. He'd create video montages as well that were scathing testimonies about popular culture, compiled from hours and hours of watching television. I look back on those tapes as a shattered mirror reflecting the absurd reality of commercial television—perhaps even the world. This wasn't someone who had a hyperactive finger on the record button; those video montages were surreal sociology.

Needless to say, because of his murals, the upset landlady eventually kicked him out. But, even better, he then found a house to live in. This place couldn't have been bigger than 700 square feet. One thing led to another, and Kurt and I started jamming. I had been playing guitar for a few years but had never been in a band. To get things moving, I picked up the bass and played through an amplifier called a PMS, of all things. It was the label on the amp, and to this day I don't know what those initials stand for with regard to musical equipment.

We found a drummer, Aaron Burckhart, and began playing constantly in that little house. We had the most intense jams. We'd simultaneously orbit inner *and* outer space. It was so serious, if we felt we sucked at rehearsal we were disappointed and we'd sit around bummed out after. It must have been about transcendence. If we didn't get that rush, that otherworldly sense of liberation, we were let down; it's hard to lose God after you've experienced it. These were not cover-song sessions or protracted blues jams. These were manifestations of a psychic dissonance.

For all its beauty, I see that dark thread through most of Kurt's creativity.

Songs started coming out of these rehearsals, and we built up a good set list. Aberdeen lacked the venues and the social network to sustain our needs as a creative entity, so we were drawn to the vitality of neighboring Olympia (Washington's state capital), home to the progressive Evergreen State College. Kurt eventually moved to Olympia proper, working nights as a janitor. Though he didn't attend school, Kurt fell in with the liberal-arts students that dominated that town. The school was a magnet for creative people. The music scene in Olympia was fiercely independent. KAOS radio played local and national underground music, and K Records held a stable of original bands. There were all kinds of events, ideas, and people, and a very leftist political element that permeated the scene.

I started working as an industrial painter and moved to Tacoma to be closer to work. Tacoma is a blue-collar town located between Olympia and Seattle. I was painting aircraft factories, aluminum and paper mills, and I joined the union doing the apprentice program. By this time the band wasn't playing much, and Kurt and I decided to ramp things up again. We found Chad Channing to join the band on drums. We built a practice studio in the basement of my rented house with discarded materials from construction sites. This was a very productive time, and the songs for our first album, *Bleach*, were coming together very well. The scene in Seattle was starting to take off too. There were shows with Mudhoney, Soundgarden, TAD, and others on the Seattle-based Sub Pop label happening all the time. Grungy guitars, sweat, and gallons of beer converged at clubs like the Vogue and the Central. The scene held together with a spirit of camaraderie, and bands were very supportive of each other. The vitality of this world contrasted sharply with the grind of working in mills. I picked up the book *On the Road* and sure enough, Kerouac struck again. I had made enough money to buy a good van; I figured that all I really needed in life was a bass guitar and the promise of the open road.

I quit my job to be a full-time starving musician. Our band was now called Nirvana and we were starting to make a name for ourselves locally and nationally. Our first album, *Bleach*, was released in June of 1989. We toured constantly, driving all over North America, playing from British Columbia, Canada to Baja California, Mexico, Montreal to Florida, Texas to Nebraska, gigging at dozens of little hole-in-the-wall clubs. I really enjoyed seeing our vast land, playing shows one town and one night at a time. Small clubs were where people on the outside of the mainstream converged. In 1989, it was inconceivable for a band like ours to be on mainstream radio—and forget about television! But there was an alternative universe, and we found it alive and well in most corners of the U.S. That fall, we toured Europe with our label-mates TAD. Europe has its differences from the U.S., but my experience proved that music is an international language—people like to rock out wherever you go. We found ourselves in Berlin the day after the wall fell. We counted a column of little Trabant cars, twenty-seven kilometers long, on the Eastern side, waiting to enter the West. The emotion of history-in-the-making was in the air. The West had much to offer and this wasn't lost on me when I noticed all of the Trabants parked on the Reeperbahn, Hamburg's notorious avenue of booze and sex.

In late 1990, Dave Grohl joined as our drummer. His contribution transformed us into a force of nature. Nirvana was now a beast that walked the earth. We toured the United Kingdom as a headliner, drawing good-sized crowds. The press started to write about us more and more. We returned to Washington for another creative and prolific period. We'd rehearse almost every night getting the material together for our second album. We were now at a point where we were selling out every venue in Seattle. And major labels were beginning to sign bands from the underground; every week brought news of another group going with the big labels. Sonic Youth and Dinosaur Jr. had been signed up, along with most of the leaders in the underground scene, as the majors scooped up the cream of the crop. Word of quarter-million-dollar contracts was common. It was a time of optimism in the music business. New technologies were embraced. The transition from vinyl to compact discs was well under way. Labels were flush with the sales of back-catalog artists in the new digital format.

It was the promise of getting paid a decent amount of money and the belief that life would be easier that motivated us to sign a major label deal. The alternative was to slog it out in the same old club scene, and the freshness and romance of that reality was starting to wear thin. We could have ramped up an independent business with all of the elements needed for a DIY operation, but we were better musicians than businessmen. We had to move forward.

In January of 1992, our second album, *Nevermind*, hit number one on the charts. This was totally unexpected. The label initially printed 50,000 copies of the record—that was supposed to last us for the next year or so. As a result of the sudden success, you couldn't find the album in any stores, but that just added to the mystique. Nirvana was truly a phenomenon. We virtually came out of nowhere and found ourselves plopped in the middle of popular culture. The album broke through with the single "Smells Like Teen Spirit." It turned into an anti-anthem that rallied the disaffected. I've always felt that the song was an observation of a culture mired in boredom amidst relative luxury. In other words, many have the means to make their own way but choose not to do so. The lyrics don't convey a literal message guiding people toward a sense of liberation. It's simply a comment on a condition.

Rock music of the late '80s had been very predictable. In 1990 no rock record had even made the top ten. *Nevermind* was the right record at the right time. Great original rock bands like R.E.M. and Jane's Addiction had previously blazed a trail to the top of the pop charts but *Nevermind* really announced the arrival of new régime. The era of the big-hair bands was over. The old bands touted merely a token rebellion; their symbols of rock 'n' roll like bandanas, whiskey bottles, and motorcycles were clichés that only created an *image* of nonconformity. The new guard held the skeptical sensibilities of the subculture along with the inherent rebellion of it all. It was real. The new guard offered meaningful rebellion, and the seismic shift that occurred in rock revealed a public that was hungry for it. It took awhile, but no longer was punk to be despised—it had landed in the mainstream, albeit neutralized by a clever use of semantics. Seattle music was referred to as "grunge," but on a national level the new movement was pigeonholed as "alternative music." I know we came out of the alternative world, but I believe the moniker of "alt-rock" was a trap set early on to control the impact of a new breed of rock 'n' roll. This way, the new music couldn't displace the status quo—it was simply labeled an alternative to it. The term *alternative* as a name for a genre of music was an instant anachronism; the name cancelled itself out. By the time alternative landed in the mainstream, the old guard had run its course, and there was no real alternative except stasis.

But the new order wasn't just about fresh music; it was also supported by the ideals and values cultivated from the punk rock world. In many ways, the grunge/alternative revolution of the early '90s was a call to consciousness. A lot of musicians really cared about equality and human rights. The old guard of big-hair bands touted a macho swagger packaged in a soft feminine look. Grunge was its symmetrical opposite. It broke through with sensitive introspection wrapped in aggression and facial hair. The revolution was inclusive, with women musicians a vital component of the scene. Feminist ideals fit naturally with the new sensibility. Political information booths became common at concerts. Bands played benefits and didn't shy from talking about issues.

In 1991, the first war with Iraq broke out. I recall being so disgusted with the whole affair. War is the most horrific of human endeavors and I've never comprehended its glorification; watching society cheer it on like a football game affirmed my status as an outsider. Odds are, the average person had never even heard of Iraq, but how quickly they lined up to join the parade of death and destruction toward an obscure, faraway nation. From the luxury of distance, war was waged to the *schlager* tune of "Tie a Yellow Ribbon Round the Old Oak Tree," a song for the troops so far from home. The phrase "We Support Our Troops" appeared on thousands of car bumpers. It was not lost on me that these vehicles needed to burn Kuwaiti oil to get down the road. I resented the notion that if you didn't support the war you didn't support the troops. I have always supported working people, and I didn't need big bellicose oil men trying to paint me into a rhetorical corner. I marched against the war with zeal, and Nirvana played a benefit concert opposing it, but the public fervor was too strong to gain any sense of balance. The enduringly nasty nuances of American foreign policy didn't matter. It was war season, and time to get on board. I was in a music store in Olympia buying some bass strings when a man in a military uniform started to make nasty jokes about Iraqi women. He was quite jovial because Hussein had been driven out of Kuwait that day. I remember glaring at him and feeling quite livid. It would probably be the same revulsion I'd have if I were forced to witness necrophilia. Thank God I had my own home and way of life for shelter from the madness.

In the spring of 1992, I was invited to a rally in Olympia. The occasion was the passage of a censorship law, and I knew the rally's organizers, leaders of an organization called the Washington Music Industry Coalition (WMIC). I showed up a little after the rally started. With the intention of just letting the organizers do their thing, I didn't plan on speaking. But being in a band with a hit record makes blending into a crowd hard. Immediately upon my arrival, reporters approached me and started asking about the law. I was startled. I must have said that I was for freedom of speech (or something like that), but otherwise I was totally unprepared. So much for just being there! I was merely the bass player in a rock band—wouldn't the press be better off talking to the people who organized the event? The organizers were way more informed on the issue than I was. Why was my opinion so important? The answer is: People were already listening to my music so naturally they wanted to know more about me. There was a real connection. People look for meaning in their music *and* their politics.

The November 1992 election resulted in the largest youth vote since 1971, the year the 26th Amendment was ratified. Youth culture, especially music media outlets like MTV and the organization Rock the Vote, served as a conduit promoting civic participation. The 26th Amendment, which lowered the voting age to eighteen, was a direct product of the role played by youth in the enduring social changes of the 1960s. We caught an echo of that populism, and in 1992 youth were credited with electing the first Democrat in twelve years. Nirvana was keenly interested in the election, beginning with the primaries. I remember admonishing Kurt for sending $200 to the Jerry Brown presidential campaign. As a rule, Brown accepted only contributions no greater than $100, so I felt anything over that would violate his ethic. Kurt just shrugged, and indeed the Brown campaign never sent the money back. In Oregon that year, Ballot Measure 9 proposed institutionalizing discrimination against gays and lesbians; Nirvana headlined a fundraiser opposing it in September 1992. We also organized a benefit in April 1993 to bring attention to the plight of women in the Balkan conflicts of the time. We used our stature for what we thought was right. In concert or on TV, we wore T-shirts of our favorite bands, hoping that the power of music would steer people toward independence. Robert Fripp of King Crimson once told me that in the late '60s, many thought music was going to save the world.

Personally and socially, things had changed in a big way for me, some for better, some for worse. It was like the whole world came knocking. I was used to stepping out into the world, but now the world wanted to come in. This didn't help the situation with Nirvana. There were many internal and external pressures. It was difficult to reconcile with the mainstream world. The change was so big and so fast. When I look back at those two and a half years of meteoric fame, it feels like it was a span of ten years. Things were so intense, so compressed. Everyone in the band dealt with the changes in his own way. In hindsight, there was a lack of skills needed to cope with the situation. Applying some kind of metaphor regarding carrying "the weight of the world" is easily overstated. I want to keep a distance from that sentiment, but as far as the music world went, there was a New Messiah. Kurt couldn't bear that, at least not alone, and in April of 1994 he killed himself.

Kurt's death was a giant media affair. Someone remarked that it was like the Kennedy assassination, but with MTV News anchor Kurt Loder in the Walter Cronkite role. The international media descended upon Seattle to report on the death of this "Spokesperson of a Generation." If he was a spokesperson, Kurt gained his mandate through an economic democracy—it's as if every album sold was a vote for Nirvana. Tragically, he picked the wrong way to resign from the position he was thrust into. A person passing away is a supernatural event. Mix this with the cultural impact of someone whose words touched so many, and you have the recipe for deity. Kurt joined the pantheon of musicians who died at their prime. All movements have their icons. Alberto Corda photographed Che Guevara in 1960 in what would become one of the most reproduced images of the 20th century. As Guevara entered the mythos of revolution, Kurt Cobain did the same for thoughtful rock 'n' roll.

The end of the band left a vacuum in the music world. Nirvana had been like an art book with bands cutting out clippings, and it didn't take long for the fickle music industry to start whining again for a new messiah. In 1997 and '98 the music business was poised for some kind of electronica/pop hybrid to usher in a new era. It never happened. Saviors are a phenomenon. They don't just materialize for the sake of moving merchandise. There is always that anticipation for the next big thing. Never mind attempting to make it happen for yourself, or making your own way. Salvation is a good thing if you can get it, and more importantly if you can hold onto it. I have learned to separate Kurt Cobain the person from Kurt Cobain the deity. There is a heavy place in my heart for the person I knew. The deity part is not my concern; that's for people who need the mystique. But watching the "deity phenomenon" at close hand has given me a greater insight into it, and this makes me ponder the human side of history's legendary people.

Whenever I'm out in public I get recognized as the "bass player of Nirvana." I am very proud of this and try to be gracious to people who approach me. So many tell me how Nirvana has changed their lives. It's heavy. I understand because I have been there. As a musician and a fan, I've experienced the power of music. Music was always there when I needed it. Nirvana, by definition, means freedom. There is no manifesto, ideology, or method to offer. I believe salvation is a personal affair. It's up to each of us to get what we want or need from it. That is why freedom of religion is so important in our nation. We have freedom *from* religion in the U.S. too. And for good reason; it prevents the overbearing from bludgeoning the sublime.

Chapter 2: Music Is Politics

In THE SUMMER OF 1994, the touring rock festival Lollapalooza considered booking its Washington State show in Hoquiam, Aberdeen's sister city. The proposal was for the show to be held in the historic Olympic Stadium, an all-wood baseball park named for the nearby mountain range. The stadium is public property; thus, in the American tradition of transparency, a public hearing was held on the issue. This was big news for a small town. To accommodate all the interested people, the hearing was moved from the city council chambers to an old movie theater. I thought Hoquiam hosting Lollapalooza was a great idea, and I decided to attend what was to be my first public hearing.

True to the high level of interest, there were a couple hundred people at the cavernous old theater. A lot of youth came to speak up for rock 'n' roll. The council sat behind tables set up on the stage, a panel of citizens who earned their authority by the consent of the city's voters. The mayor sat in the center. A veteran schoolteacher, she took control of the meeting by calling the fidgeting crowd of chatty music fans to order. The people's business started under the ornate plaster of the hushed theater. Before the concert issue came up, citizens had the opportunity to address other matters. One gentleman who looked like he must have rode over on a Harley-Davidson stood up and raised his hand. He stated that his street had many children and the city should install a "Slow" traffic sign for safety. The council promised to look into it.

Finally, with all other business completed, the festival came up for discussion. Many people stood and voiced their support. I felt, as a "famous son" of Grays Harbor County, I could also say a few words. I voiced my support for the concert, but I wanted to take the opportunity to clear some things up too. Aberdeen and Grays Harbor took a lot of knocks for being in some kind of horrible area, pasted in mythology as the place where Kurt Cobain was, for lack of a better word, tortured. I spoke about how Nirvana had traveled the world and that we saw a little bit of Grays Harbor in most places we went. The good and the bad can easily be picked out of anywhere.

Testifying at the hearing was like my experience attending the Olympia censorship rally a few years earlier. I had more than my share of attention. It's as if my words were succeeded with, *"Thus spoke the rock star!"*—so it goes when you spread the gospel of rock 'n' roll. I felt the most compelling testimony came from a young man who, I would bet, was at his first public hearing too. He raised his hand, stood up, and in a very nervous voice said, "Can't you give us a chance?" He must have figured he'd said all he could, because he sat right back down. It was the kind of sincerity found off the jaded, beaten path. I knew what he was talking about. The quaint Olympic Stadium in Hoquiam, Washington would be the center of the music universe for a day. Indeed, heaven on earth!

Like the traffic sign, the council promised to consider the idea. There were many realities that then came into play. The old wooden rafters of the stadium would be strained. The city's population would quadruple for a day, so public safety and the number of personnel needed to work the event were important considerations. In the end, the machinations of the music-promotion business weighed in, and Hoquiam lost the competition.

The hearing was another beautiful manifestation of the nation functioning in the manner envisioned by our founders. A city council has the obligation to consider issues affecting the common good. This is ensured by the governmental devises granted us. In other words, if any of the councilors refuse their obligations, come election day, we can try to throw the bums out!

Unalienable Nation

ON JULY 4, 1776, our founders declared their independence. In the course of this declaration, they revealed the philosophy of our nation:

> All men are created equal, that they are endowed by their Creator with certain unalienable rights; that among these are Life, Liberty, and the pursuit of Happiness. That, to secure these rights, Governments are instituted among Men, deriving their just powers from the consent of the governed. That whenever any Form of Government becomes destructive of these ends, it is the Right of the People to alter or to abolish it, and to institute new Government . . .

A central idea, or philosophy, of the U.S. is that the governed and the government are one and the same. That's why we're always having elections. Every year, from local utility boards and municipal offices, from state legislatures to the office of president, we, as a people, have a say in our government's direction.

But democracy doesn't end on election day. We have many opportunities to engage our system. I recognized, on that afternoon at the council meeting, that public hearings are an exercise in participation just as important as voting. We are afforded so many opportunities in the U.S. to work toward the common good.

Erotic Music Laws

MY HOME STATE had a penchant for laws and regulations that would impact the music industry in a negative way. I've seen the heights that Northwest music can soar to, and was annoyed that we were getting so much disrespect from our lawmakers. We couldn't sit around and wait for something to save us—we had to make our own way. The state wanted to impose what could be considered an apartheid system on music.

The Erotic Music Law, first passed in 1992, turned the notion of American justice upside down. It gave prosecutors the power to deem music "unfit for minors." A prosecutor in some remote county could mount a censorship crusade affecting the whole state. If a record fell under the ruling, it couldn't be displayed in front of minors. A sticker in forty-eight-point type stating, "Adults Only," had to be placed on the cover. It could be stuck in the "adult" section of a record store. Even worse, the record would carry the stigma of being "adult material" and might be banished by retailers, clearing the way toward "adult music stores"! Of course, an artist could avoid all this by changing his or her lyrics, but that's another aspect of censorship—the chilling effect. Musicians would have to go to court and prove that their art wasn't obscene, and that was the point of the law—you were guilty until proven innocent.

Statutes like the Erotic Music Law are attractive to law-makers. Censorship laws appear to address the problems affecting youth and even society as a whole. If a troubled young person shoots up his or her school, it's easy to blame it on a rock or rap band. Teen pregnancy can be explained by suggestive lyrics. Emotional despair, neglect, feelings of emptiness, or just plain ignorance are issues that require a lot of time and energy to tackle. Solutions to these deep problems can cost money. It's easier, and cheaper, to lay the blame elsewhere.

In 1998, I had the opportunity to testify in front of the U.S. Senate. It was a hearing of the Commerce Committee. The issue was the negative effect of popular music on young people. There was a teacher from Arkansas who worked at a school that had experienced the tragedy of a mass shooting. It was hard watching her testify. She told the committee how before the incident, the shooter had made his threats in a nice way; he would say, "Yes ma'am," or, "Yes sir." It's as if they couldn't hear the music, so to speak.

I knew that Marilyn Manson was wrongly blamed by some people for influencing the horrible atrocities at Columbine High School in Colorado. When a senator brought up Manson, I told him and the committee that I had been to one of his concerts and had left impressed with what I considered serious political speech. Manson sings songs about alienation and hypocrisy, and whatever you think about him, he's *not* saying one thing and doing another —in sharp contrast to many people at the highest levels of leadership in our nation. There is too much spin-doctoring and mud-slinging going on in politics these days. So it's not surprising that when the youth of America look for the truth, they find it in Marilyn Manson!

There was a loud gasp in the hearing room after I lobbed that one at the committee.

Soundgarden vs. Eickenberry

THE MUSIC COMMUNITY is a ripe target for onerous regulation. Musicians, and the environment around music, are notoriously antiestablishment. Most musicians wouldn't even dream of attending a public hearing. The subculture is just that—people under the surface, off the radar, making their own world. If there is little resistance to music censorship from musicians, then why not try to implement it? Whether it becomes law or not, it's a win-win situation for those who seek reelection. Lawmakers don't need to care what people think, they only need to care what *voters* think. Election advertising is geared toward voters. (Why waste money on people who don't vote?) A lot of campaign literature is aimed at suburban moms who rightly need to be concerned about what their children are up to. It's easy for candidates to say they're protecting youth with a few words in a glossy brochure.

Due to the efforts of many great people and organizations, a resistance to the Erotic Music Law came into existence. Seattle music wasn't under the radar anymore. We had international acclaim. We had to step up. The Washington Music Industry Coalition, along with the American Civil Liberties Union and the Recording Industry Association of America (RIAA), mounted a legal challenge to the law. The top of the complaint read like a who's who of the Seattle music scene. Referred to as *Soundgarden vs. Eickenberry*, the list included myself, Sir Mix-A-Lot, Pearl Jam, members of Heart, and many others. The law really did go against the basic notion of our justice system, and on November 20, 1992, Judge Mary Wicks Brucker declared it unconstitutional because, in the words of the case summary, "the statute was void on its face for vagueness; and that it constituted a prior restraint on speech in violation of the federal and state constitutions because it did not provide adequate notice to persons who might be prosecuted under its provisions and because it allowed a judge to decide what is fundamentally a jury question."

In 1995, the Erotic Music Law was resurrected and given a new name. The "Harmful to Minors" bill was very close to the same law we defeated in 1992. The bill's sponsors tweaked the language to attempt constitutional muster and brought it back with a vengeance. Both the state Senate and House passed the bill. Our only weapon at that point was our governor, Mike Lowry. We knew Governor Lowry was a strong advocate of freedom of expression and that we could count on him for a veto. But things weren't actually that simple. The legislature had just overturned his veto of another bill regarding state finances, and the same thing could happen again. We weren't about to sit around and expect a successful veto. Common decency dictated that we should support our pro-freedom governor.

I knew my situation as a well-known musician could open doors for me, so we decided to hit the legislature. Our plan was to lobby enough senators to defeat an override. That meant getting to just over a third of them. The bill had passed with such a wide margin, we even needed to ask some of those who had voted for it if they'd consider standing with us. I started working with WMIC director Richard White, and we hooked up with RIAA lobbyist Stuart Halsan. Stuart, a former state legislator, was a mentor during our crash course in civics. With his experience and connections, he not only showed us around the capitol physically, he showed us the ropes on how to get things done. I learned about the journey of bills. It was a cold plunge into our political process. We walked the lobbies of the capitol and met with lawmakers, presenting the case for music in our state. We were propelled by a proactive message. We stood for freedom of speech, and also made the point that the music industry brought cultural and economic vitality to our region. We propagated our deeply held belief that our music community is an asset, not a liability.

Enough senators pledged to protect the veto. We informed the governor, and he duly vetoed it. The Senate called for an override and it failed. Once again, freedom of expression triumphed in Washington State. RIAA president Hilary Rosen came to Olympia with special commemorative gold records that we presented to the lawmakers who had helped us preserve freedom.

America Delivers

IT WAS VERY GRATIFYING to be able to affect change. Fighting for what you believe is right is rewarding in itself, but actually achieving victory is extra special. I felt a rush of joy. There was also a profound realization. I had come a long way from my disaffected punk rock days. I realized that those same ideals of independence and nonconformity are well-suited for engaging our democracy. This made me rethink the way I looked at some fundamental issues.

I used to believe much of punk's rhetoric arguing for the wholesale abandonment of institutions, the logic being that our government is the source of injustice so it must be the problem. My mistake was that I confused hypocrisy, abuse of power, and the exclusion bred by our broken elections with our democratic system. (Similarly, I've heard too many people disparage free enterprise because they confuse it with greed and corruption. There is a difference.) I had wrongly separated myself from my government. These days, too many citizens are making the same mistake. I realized that our democracy could be inclusive.

Advocating on behalf of a constituency of music fans opened a lot of doors. The wheels of democracy turn slowly, but you can find satisfaction and make progress if you approach it the right way. Demonstrating in front of your city hall or legislature is a good way of expressing yourself. Though lacking the spontaneous excitement of a street march, testifying at a public hearing is another opportunity to constructively get something off your chest. Regardless of the approach, the idea is to address attempts at tyranny in the nonviolent context of the democratic process. That's what the U.S. is supposed to be about.

Smash the State

SOME FANTASIZE that the only course of action is to overthrow our government. What a dangerous proposition! One need only look abroad at places that lack the rule of law to dispel this notion. Imagine if the rights granted us by our Constitution were suspended. Mob rule is an ugly situation. In too many places on our planet, armed gangsters terrorize people with extortion, robbery, and summary executions. They derive power from their guns. Far better to work to make democracy live up to its name: truly representing all of us.

In 1999, I attended the demonstrations against the World Trade Organization (WTO) ministerial meeting in Seattle. Tens of thousands of people marched peacefully, exercising their rights as Americans. (Conversely, the WTO's rules undermine our respective federal and state constitutions. County and city charters are effectively nullified by the rulings of a secret tribunal. By all means, people should be in the streets screaming about this abdication of our sovereignty!) I recall thousands of citizens marching for equitable trade agreements, protection of our environment, and the strengthening of our democratic processes. The statement most often heard that day was, "This is what democracy looks like!" As freedom provides the means, there was plenty of room for artistic expression too. Street corners brimmed with political theater, music, giant puppets, and other props. Downtown Seattle seemed like a carnival.

This was all quite uplifting, but eventually a dark shroud started to descend over the city and a misbegotten few took advantage of the situation. As the day wore on, more and more windows were being smashed. More and more walls were spray-painted. Lines between the police and the public were drawn by armored police looking like Robocops, standing shoulder to shoulder across the width of a street. Many other areas were completely lawless, with the mounting destruction a sad reminder of the lack of responsibility that breeds in such a vacuum. I witnessed a person writing graffiti on the side of a hotel. I yelled at him, "How would you like it if someone did that to your house?" A couple of people who were cheering him on turned to me and said, "Fuck you!" I informed them that this was supposed to be a nonviolent protest and that vandalism is violence toward property. My comment was returned with more foul-mouthed sentiments. Of course, as a free-speech advocate I would defend his right to curse at me, but such mindless hostility is rude and counterproductive. By that point, I was so disgusted I left for home.

Thank God all I had to endure was name-calling. I could have had the daylights beaten out of me. There is an infamous photo of a guy in Nike shoes violently kicking down the letters atop the door of the Nike shop. Even some police got out of hand. Like the tear gas seeping out of police barricades, violence of all forms polluted the air. Armchair rebels dream of putsch as some kind of romantic triumph for their ideology. And who would lead the new régime? The revolutionary romantics, of course! But in reality, rogue militia with guns would march the dreamers up to the hills to dig their own graves before delivering the *coup de grâce* to the backs of their skulls.

I was jeered, but the antidemocratic words of the WTO

still stand while the graffiti on that wall has long since been scrubbed off. That's a good example of how meaningful work takes time. All the violence and incoherent expression turned out to be a distraction from important international issues. News coverage focused on the hooded, so-called anarchist troublemakers dueling with the Robocops. The fact is, credible protesters spent months organizing lawful demonstrations. Organized labor's showing in the streets made a powerful statement, and the Clinton administration took notice. The U.S. trade delegation insisted on labor issues that smaller nations with lesser standards refused to accept, and as a result the negotiations collapsed. It was the enduring role of the trade unions and their impact on electoral politics that made the difference, not the transient, spontaneous actions of vandals literally out for kicks.

On December 1, the day after the major demonstrations, Jello Biafra, Kim Thayil, Gina Mainwal, and I played a one-off protest concert, which is documented on the album *The No WTO Combo Live from the Battle in Seattle.*

Politics Are Conventional

STARTING A PRO-MUSIC political action committee (PAC) was considered unconventional. But many businesses create this kind of entity to work on their behalf; why should the local music business be any different? A PAC is an entity created under federal rules for special interests to support candidates or political parties for election. The Joint Artists and Music Promotions Political Action Committee (JAMPAC) was conceived in 1995 as an organization to get a message out and protect the interests of people who add to the greater good. We supported pro-music candidates for public office. We identified issues that had a negative impact on our community and took them on. We repeated over and over again that our music community brings cultural and economic vitality to our state. It's that simple because it's the truth.

On a local level, the music scene is one part of a community's arts scene. But compared to other artistic disciplines, popular music doesn't really have patrons, subsidies, or grants from public or nonprofit entities. Most music commerce involves independent businesspeople working in the free enterprise system. There is a whole economy built around the phenomenon of music. Take, for example, a band of eighteen-year-olds. If they want to go out and play professionally, they are essentially a small business. They need capital to pay for equipment and services. They need to cover their liabilities. They are subject to regulations and they pay taxes under a business structure. Who determines the extent and impact of all this? The legislature. So when people tell me that politics has no place in music, I think about the reality of the situation. Done well, politics can work *with* the creative side of music. And as far as the commercial side goes, all I can say is: Democracy is everybody's business.

For over a decade, the Seattle music scene endured a law called the Teen Dance Ordinance (TDO). The TDO was a classic example of throwing out the baby with the bath water. It was an overreaction to a bad situation that occurred in the mid-'80s with an all-ages club that was run very irresponsibly. The place was a haven for runaways, drug abuse, and exploitative sex. It was a problem for the whole community. The city decided it could fix things with a sweeping law that regulated teen dances. The law was broadly written, but there were many loopholes and enforcement was selective. The law's language resulted in a lot of uncertainty, thus chilling enthusiasm for all-ages events.

Our problems were not limited to teen dances. Our state's liquor laws prohibited minors and even adults between the ages of eighteen and twenty access to small-scale music events. If our music industry does have a "subsidy," it is the sale of alcohol. It's common for a venue to split the proceeds of an evening, with the bands receiving the door charge and the club keeping the income from the bar. I've played all over the United States and seen many different arrangements for keeping alcohol out of the hands of minors; Washington State had some of the most exclusive rules in the nation. Where would popular music be without young people? Youth are our future. It's part of nature's grand plan. If Seattle and the Northwest are to continue our legacy of musical vitality, we need to include people of all ages in our music scene.

Things had to change. We applied our proactive message with some hard, cold facts. We recognized the serious responsibility the State Liquor Control Board has in regulating the drug, alcohol. It was not our intention to interfere with that. We only wanted to expand access to music, not alcohol consumption. We knew we couldn't have a vibrant music community without safety. Our message of economic vitality was very important too. Small music venues mostly employ young people. Like any small business they require goods and services. Taxes are collected on every admission ticket sold at these events. We proposed meeting a need for safe and supervised all-ages events while adding to the tax coffers and local economy in the process. *Do I see a miracle?*

We eventually drew enough attention to the issue that a special task force was created by the city. People like David Meinert, a Seattle music promoter, and Angel Combs, a political activist, worked for eighteen months in good faith with the Seattle city council, police and fire departments, the city attorney's office, and parents toward a solution. In the end, the TDO was repealed. But many parents and people in leadership still felt we needed some rules to apply to all-ages shows. Our music scene realized that to move forward, we needed to compromise on some issues. With the ensuing concessions, the city passed the All Ages Dance Ordinance. It is reasonable, and most importantly, it's working. It was tempting to shoot for all or nothing. But democracy doesn't work that way. Consensus gave us what we wanted anyway—an inclusive music scene.

The Grind

SUCCEEDING IN THE FACE of the slow grind of the democratic process is a wonderful experience. Politics can be tremendously tedious and frustrating. The average person is adverse to change; people get scared when you suggest they step out of their comfort zone. Regardless of how many are affected by bad laws or regulations, people fear change by nature and often avoid taking chances. We were only advocating for the inclusion of people of all ages at music shows. But those opposed to changes put forth doomsday scenarios—they made it sound like we wanted to repeal all the laws that dealt with statutory rape and alcohol consumption. Hysteria, by the sheer weight of its emotional effect, will push aside the rational. This can impede progress toward change. One must stick to a positive message to overcome this challenge. Many elected officials are mired in the throes of ideology or theology. A rational appeal will fall on deaf ears to those who only see through the lens of their cause.

The political process cannot be an exclusive club (even though it often seems like one). All have the right to participate, for better or worse. A hearing is a worthy exercise in governmental transparency. But like many human endeavors, hearings can be faulted. They can test a person's patience too. A lot of public testimony is an expression of tortured logic crammed through a sieve of bad writing skills. I've sat through long sessions only to have the time run out before I had an opportunity to speak. Some people go to hearings as if they have nothing better to do. These regulars always offer testimony full of digressions. Some have chips on their shoulders and never fail in getting contentious with a committee. So mired in their own convictions, they are oblivious that their personal crusades are cluttering the process.

There is a difference between meaningful work and crusading. Meaningful work takes time. Advocating on behalf of the interests of the music community is usually not a life-and-death struggle. All too often satisfaction is elusive, but if you have your eyes on the prize, you won't let the slow wheels of democracy grind you down. If you know you're doing the best work you can, with the best people, that's all you can do. People who do meaningful work know the right moment to take a break, because tomorrow offers a new day to make a positive contribution to society. Crusaders, on the other hand, are addicted to the rush of their issue. They'll often plow forward and not stop until, they hope, their issue is realized. Crusaders usually work alone or in very small groups. They often disparage other people who have views similar to their own. This is because the crusader only knows one way—theirs!

I believe each person should determine what level of political participation feels most comfortable for him or her. I don't want to live all over anybody and expect them to jump into politics; I'll leave that to the overbearing crusaders. There are good people willing to do the heavy lifting, and I ask you to please support them the best you can. Politics can be an irrational terrain with the lumps and bumps jarring your psyche. But it's the rough ride that makes a winning finish all the more sweet. If anything, the biggest accomplishment is the victory over cynicism. Cynics dismiss any effort to change things; in effect, they embrace the status quo even while refuting it. Believe me, I have been to the depths of cynicism. Politics breeds it. But cynicism's pit is an illusion. It's an easy trap to fall into, but it can disappear simply by recognizing the positive. The positive ideal holds an appealing dignity. Why kick around the argument of being *against* censorship when you can advocate *for* freedom of expression? Why *disparage* violence when you can *promote* peace? Essentially, the positive ideal is about advancing the possibilities.

Chapter 3: Flip-Flop Patriots

NO RECENT EVENT has scarred the national psyche like the terror attacks of September 11, 2001. While there are many things that divide us, following the attacks we came together, as a nation, for the common purpose of unity. We were bloodied but unbowed, refusing to accept that such an attack would tear us down. The ruins of the World Trade Center were "Ground Zero" to a nation's trauma. The period following that tragedy was marked by a tremendous swell of patriotism. The slogan "United We Stand" adorned paraphernalia from T-shirts to bumper stickers. Although many hold a sincere faith, it never fails for the trinket peddlers to be found on the path to an apparition site or shrine. A cottage industry arose from the ashes of tragedy.

But while patriotism was strong on the streets, a deeper look beneath the surface revealed that we really stood divided. The November 2002 election was an opportunity to exercise the most fundamental of our civic duties—all our state legislatures and both houses of the U.S. Congress held elections. Flags were flying high. We had invaded a nation in the name of democracy. The virtues of patriotism were being extolled constantly, permeating the national psyche. But when the call came to walk the walk, most Americans turned away. Voter turnout in 2002 was a scant 40%! On that second Tuesday of November, most of the electorate declined to say "yes" to the very *idea* of the U.S.A.

The notion that our leaders derive their powers from the consent of the governed obviously seemed meaningless to many. This was a jarring dichotomy with opinion polls that showed the overwhelming majority of citizens approved the government's reaction to the 9/11 atrocities. Citizens could, at least, have cast a simple vote to convey some kind of mandate or affirmation to our leaders. It was a time of glee, though, for Republicans, who retook the whole federal government. Which just goes to show, regardless of the disgraceful turnout, nothing succeeds like success. The Democrats tried hard to ride the nationalism bandwagon. It was proclaimed by the President, in the name of national unity, that you were either with us or you were with the terrorists. Refusing to fall for this rhetorical trap by choosing neither proposition was the route toward the wilderness far away from the incessant drumbeat of nationalism.

By the summer preceding the '02 elections, cracks in the collective fervor had started to appear. Patriotic paraphernalia was piling up on discount racks. Surplus T-shirts, stickers, and other knickknacks were now reduced in price for quick sale. How symbolic this was of the tragedy of November 2002, when nearly two-thirds of the nation discounted their democracy. On that election day, the swell of patriotism seemed reduced to the size of a tattered little flag that's been on a car antenna for too long.

I was in a supermarket when I noticed just how out of hand the nationalism business had become. There, in the middle of a patriotic marketing display, was a pair of American-flag flip-flop sandals. I couldn't believe how insensitive this was to the symbol of the United States. I bet they would sell like hotcakes at an anti-American rally in Islamabad. I started to wonder what would happen if I burned a flag in front of that store. I bet there would've been a brawl. And chances are I would have been stomped by feet wearing those Old Glory flip-flops!

I go to many civic events, both public and private. It's routine for me to salute the American flag and recite the Pledge of Allegiance with my fellow citizens. I have no problem using the words "under God" either. As far as that issue goes, I am making a reference to my personal god. Although I've never noticed anybody abstaining from the Pledge or the religious reference, I wouldn't have a problem if they did. It would be un-American to compel anybody, of any age, to align themselves with something they didn't agree with.

But in the outpouring of patriotism in post-9/11 America, the notion of minding your own business is unfathomable. On April 27, 2004, Democratic Seattle congressman Jim McDermott omitted the words "under God" while leading the U.S. House in the Pledge. I don't know McDermott's personal faith, and I don't care—that's his business. But it was blasphemous to his colleagues. These legislators, who swore to uphold the Constitution, somehow forgot about the 1st Amendment. He got a reprimand from the leader of his own party. The fearful dished out the public spanking to cut loose the liability of having one of their own invite the wrath of the "more patriotic than thou" crowd. Never mind the low turnout in our elections and rampant cynicism— those who exhibit their independence are slapped down by scoundrels draped in red, white, and blue. And the self-righteous are waiting and watching, ready to pile on anyone who steps out of line. This not only serves their political agenda, the denunciations also provide content to fill the airtime between advertisements on for-profit news/propa-ganda media.

I own an American flag and I'm quite fond of it. It's an older one with forty-eight stars. It is stitched together and holds the weight of quality craftsmanship. If anybody were to take it from me I would try to stop them. It's my flag and it's part of my home. It has meaning for me. It symbolizes a land where people aren't compelled to march in lockstep to the drumbeat of idolatry.

In Seattle, there is a large statue of Vladimir Lenin standing right in the middle of the kitschy Fremont district. It used to stand somewhere in Eastern Europe, but was discarded by people who needed to purge themselves of the crushing dogma of the forgers of the statue (of course, that's just my own speculation). Here in the U.S., we can read into the monument whatever we want to. We can stand in front of the statue with signs denouncing it. Or we can stand in praise, advocating the ideas of Lenin. People can stop and listen. They can ignore us or tell us why we're wrong. In the old U.S.S.R., you could never erect a statue of George Washington or Abraham Lincoln. The mere mention of this would have sent you off to the gulag as an enemy of the homeland.

You'd think the low turnout in the 2002 election would be cause for alarm. And let's not forget the 2000 election fiasco either. These are events that make us the laughing stock of a world that likes to see the big guy fall. What about enjoying a vital democracy where the overwhelming majority of citizens participate? Forget it! Many in Congress believe we need an amendment to our Constitution prohibiting burning the flag. They believe it necessary, because we must protect "what America stands for." And what if we did pass this amendment? What would stop dissenters from burning copies of our Constitution at demonstrations? I believe this would be a fitting gesture toward a document that bars freedom of expression. Go burn the Chinese flag in Tiananmen Square and see what happens. Or burn an American flag in front of the Chinese factory that makes them. You'd probably have only enough time to pass out a few copies of the Bill of Rights before the police came to arrest you.

Wasted Voters

WORKING ON POLITICAL ISSUES involves talking to a lot of people. In the course of advocating issues, I've learned that a message has more weight when it speaks on behalf of real people. *That's what democracy is all about.* Having a constituency on your side *does* make a difference to lawmakers.

I've spoken to many people about the benefits of inclusion and fairness. While there was much enthusiasm with regard to specific issues and the process of moving legislation, when it came to talking about voting, many started to cool. I can't tell you how many times I've heard people tell me they felt like their vote didn't count, or that they were wasting their vote. I have always tried to be positive. I'd go on about how every vote does count, and how it's our duty as Americans to participate. But it didn't take long to sink in that I was just pitching platitudes. This caused me a crisis of faith. Here I was, the bass player/politician espousing the wonderful attributes of our democracy, but maybe I was carrying some illusory idealism. I started to feel like I had suckered myself. I couldn't go out into the notoriously skeptical and antiestablishment music community and pitch people that they "just gotta believe!" People find meaning in music, but they are surely not finding it in their democracy. "Democracy is everybody's business," I'd explain, but I couldn't get the message through. What a shame that for so many people voting is meaningless.

The search for meaning is a fundamental principal of our human experience. Democracy is supposed to be passionate. It's no mistake that a political event is referred to as a *rally*. Our nation has always succeeded when we rise to the challenge of working toward the common good, but our two-party system dampens enthusiasm and artificially divides us into two camps. Too many voters resign themselves to a defeatist perspective; they vote for the lesser of two evils. Voters daring to challenge that system, like those voting for Ross Perot in 1992 or Ralph Nader in 2000, are slapped down as spoilers.

The more I thought about the high rate of nonparticipation, the more I felt it was the result of a political structure that discourages diverse ideas. Just as the world of music in the '90s was crying out for "alternative rock," it seems that politics today needs a way for alternative political voices to play a genuine role in politics instead of being marginalized by "pragmatic" political pros.

But it's no coincidence that people are not participating. There is a culture of discouragement around our elections. It strikes at the heart of the very notion of independence. Anyone who considers running outside our two-party system is usually not taken seriously. The cold, hard reality is that third-party candidates are often wasting their own and everybody else's time. Yes, there can be idealistic candidates who want to make a statement. And the choice between the two major candidates could be unpalatable enough for some to be forced to vote their conscience—but don't often expect to get someone elected.

A few Independents do get elected here and there, but that's the exception and not the rule. Within a two-party system, coalitions are built *before* an election. Interest groups identify either a Republican or Democratic candidate and support them. Third parties, and those who would like to support them, are forced to learn from successful special interests and cast their lot with one of the major parties. Special interests commonly hedge their bets by contributing to incumbents from both major parties. This provides no incentive for corporations and individual high donors to contribute to non-incumbent third-party campaigns. This is the foundation of our American political duopoly. The U.S.S.R. shipped off those who didn't comply with their one-party rule to the gulag of the Arctic wilderness. While the situation is not by any means as severe in the U.S., third parties are still exiled to the media/political wilderness outside of our two-party system. The damning fact being that they worked against candidates and parties in control. This can make the halls of government difficult territory. In a two-party system, the score is settled on election day, and the power rests with the elected members of government. To advance issues, special interests work with lawmakers during their campaigns and legislative sessions.

Third parties may have legitimate philosophical differences with the two major parties. Starting a political organization independent of the establishment is fundamental to the right of free association. This is supposed to be the cornerstone of democracy—and freedom itself! But our elections don't accommodate third parties by design. The will of the majority can be upset when there are three candidates in an election. Our two-party system is a crude reflection of the political right and left. But politics are not black and white; many voters inhabit the grey area between the ideological poles.

There are three kinds of Independents; first, those who are genuinely caught in the middle between Democrats and Republicans, so-called "centrists." A second kind of

Independents are people who literally do not know the difference between Democrats and Republicans because they are turned off by the dull, safe style of spokespeople for both major parties. Voters are constantly subjected to candidates talking platitudes about how they stand for job creation, greater access to health care, and better education, while not sharing any specifics. Finally, there are Independents who have strong views that neither major party is expressing. The first group tends to decide at the last minute for a Republican or Democrat. The other two groups sometimes follow suit, sometimes decline to vote, and sometimes emerge when given the opportunity to vote for candidates such as Ross Perot, Jesse Ventura, and Ralph Nader.

Opinion polls show that a full third of Americans consider themselves Independents. But a quick survey of the political landscape shows that true Independents, or individuals who refuse party affiliation down the line, are few and far between in public office—only six among our nearly 8,000 state legislators and members of Congress. This centrist demographic of Independents is also referred to as "swing voters." Swing voters are coveted by the two major parties in the few competitive legislative elections held anymore. They're given names to identify their perceived lifestyles; research shows that "soccer moms" or "NASCAR dads" can vote either way. These voters gain disproportionate attention in the form of lip service or actual movement on governmental policy. Both major parties are competing over the same constituency, thus they have to espouse similar themes. This is a factor in the complaint that there is no major difference between Democrats and Republicans. The two major parties can afford to throw a lot of resources at swing groups because they have their ideological core constituencies in the bag, only needing to motivate them to vote by instilling fear that the other party is the "greater evil." Under current electoral rules, the only option for voters who decline to join the pre-election coalition is the third-party wilderness.

But having said all this, even with our current electoral rules, a viable third party could very well emerge in the U.S. This might be hastened by the defection of either Democratic or Republican officeholders. Bolstered by their name recognition, voting record, and fundraising experience, these renegade legislators could actually give the major parties a run for their money. In our first-place-takes-all system, a viable third party candidate might only need a 34% plurality to win an election.

Most third-party or independent candidates rarely poll in the double digits—Ross Perot's 19% in 1992 was a rare exception. But in a close election, a third party could spoil it for the majority with just a 5% showing. A district or state could contain a center-left ideological majority, but still lose due to a split constituency. In 2000, the combined center-left/Gore-Nader vote total was more than 51% but the Republicans won with less than 48%; Green candidate Ralph Nader cut into the left coalition, thus spoiling the election for the Democrats. This has also happened in New Mexico, where Green party legislative candidates have polled in double digits and the center-left majority gets split; in 1997 and '98, the GOP won in special elections where Green candidates got three times more votes than the margin of victory (one race was 44-39-14). (The tragic joke in New Mexico is that GREEN means: Get Republicans Elected Every November.) In the 2000 Washington U.S. Senate race, third parties tipped the balance in the other direction; incumbent Republican Slade Gorton lost votes to the Libertarian candidate, while Democrat Maria Cantwell picked up Nader voters because the Greens didn't run a candidate. Cantwell's victory can be attributed to the center-left coalition staying intact to rally around a single candidate.

Most political media only cover the horserace between the two major-party candidates. If an outside candidate does gain attention, it's because they're considered spoilers. Ralph Nader has been derided for his 2000 presidential candidacy, and since then has suffered as the scapegoat for Gore losing the election. On February 22, 2004, he announced his intention to run again as an Independent. Democrats all across the nation gasped, "Not again!" They even protested outside of the television studio where he appeared that day. Prominent Democrats called him an egotist, conveniently ignoring poll numbers that showed one in nine young people wanted to vote for him despite the obvious odds against him winning. Many Republicans chortled, welcoming this fortunate advantage for them. Our broken democracy sets the stage for such reactions. Nader's candidacy is once again seen as a liability, potentially splitting the center-left constituency.

Many cries for reform came out of the 2000 election, but meaningful solutions to the spoiler phenomenon go ignored. Nader is the canary in the coalmine; most just want to kill the little bird, while our democracy teeters in peril. Why are we picking on Ralph Nader? Anybody who is eligible is supposed to have the right to run for office in our nation—especially when his views on issues like the war in Iraq, fair trade, and consumer protection from corporations are different than either major-party candidate. Shouldn't a functioning democracy celebrate diversity of opinion and inclusion? Not in our U.S.A. Nader is being slapped down like a bad little boy only because he wishes to be president and challenges the two-party consensus on major issues. But third-party and Independent candidates that poll like Nader do exhibit a minority-rule phenomenon, of sorts, in the way they affect elections. Nader could get the Democrats to make concessions in order to get him to play ball with the center-left team. (But perhaps I'm being too rational.)

What a shame that in the United States of America, some *voters* are considered nothing less than a liability too. If many are mad at Nader, what about those who will vote for him? We should not presume whose votes belong to whom. Too many people obviously do. It's overbearing to expect someone to vote for a candidate that's unappealing to them. And it gets worse; some people see the "spoiler vote" phenomenon as an opportunity. In Washington State, a Republican Party operative went so far as to recruit Green Party activists to run for office. He called up the Greens and offered to shepherd them through the whole process of getting on the ballot, even paying filing fees. The Greens started to notice something fishy when this person would invite them to business lunches at greasy spoon diners, then smoke cigarettes and order roast beef sandwiches. He was found out and the Greens gave the money back.

In the 2002 California gubernatorial race, Republican candidate Bill Simon invited Green candidate Peter Camejo to a debate. Democratic candidate Gray Davis would have none of it; he refused to debate if the Green was included and it turned into another spoiler story for the media. But was Simon practicing the inclusive fundamentals of true democracy? Did he want to broaden the discourse for the benefit of voters? No way! Simon wanted to split the left sphere and tilt the election to his favor, and Davis knew it. The *Los Angeles Times,* which sponsored the debate, excluded Camejo because of the newspaper's own threshold for candidates to poll at least 15%. This put the Green in a Catch-22. Camejo could possibly have polled 15%, or even higher, if he'd had better coverage. If he was included in the debate, and debated well, he also might have reached that threshold; he might at least have been able to double the 5% he was polling at the time. Regardless, the two-party conventional wisdom prevailed, and the debate was duly narrowed.

House Odds

INCUMBENT POLITICIANS have many built-in advantages. Their record has constant exposure to voters. Their ability to vote publicly on legislation attracts special interests and the funds they contribute to a campaign. Incumbents generally don't have to worry about primary challenges and can just focus on winning the general election. Proving you can do a good job as a public servant is also an advantage well-deserved.

Another advantage most candidates enjoy—similar to the house odds in a casino—is that most regions of the country favor one major party over the other, a division graphically shown by the maps with red "Republican" territory and blue 'Democratic" territory (which in my state plays out with Democrats sweeping almost all seats in the Seattle area, and Republicans dominating the eastern half of the state). That natural partisan advantage is boosted by having districts drawn to benefit particular incumbents and their parties. In the fairest games, the odds are around 50/50. But the reality in this "game" is that the odds are stacked against too many voters.

Every ten years, after the release of the Census, lawmakers from the incumbent Democratic and Republican parties carve out new legislative districts. In essence, they pick the voters before the voters pick them. This is the notion of democracy turned upside down. The incumbent parties cushion their safe seats with sophisticated polling and demographic techniques that rig a district to their favor. Redistricting is a tawdry affair. It is where political-survival instincts trump the ideal of democracy or even decency. It is a blood sport where voters are the pawns. Lawmakers essentially gain the almost divine power of deciding who merits representation and who doesn't. Like some kind of geographic lottery, citizens are included or excluded from their legislature by virtue of where they live. This is so engrained in our mentality that legislative districts are even referred to as either Democratic or Republican, depending on how the lines fall. It's like saying, "Your candidate can't win because you live in a Democratic district," or vice versa. You'd think that legislative districts and their representatives would belong to the citizens who inhabit them, and not private political organizations.

Early in the history of the United States, those in power discovered the political benefits of drawing up districts. The word "gerrymander" was first used in 1812 when the governor of Massachusetts, Elbridge Gerry, created an election district that looked like a salamander. Gerrymandered districts have all kinds of tortuous shapes. Some are like the letter K or X. Some wind like an S, resembling a serpent. Redistricting is not about looking out for democracy, it's about incumbent parties looking out for themselves. The party in power will "pack" a district full of supportive voters, or they'll "crack" or split another full of potential opposition. Democrats and Republicans muscle each other out in whatever state they enjoy the upper hand. In Texas in 2003, Republicans figuratively chased out the Democrats through redistricting. In retaliation, the Texas Democrats famously vamoosed from the state in an attempt to scuttle the gerrymander. They eventually got burned out with hiding in motels rooms and returned, ensuring victory for the Republican majority in the legislature. The politically liberal city of Austin was "cracked" between three elongated Republican districts that run for hundreds of miles. Some Austin voters will share a district with San Antonio, while neighbors across the street will be in another district connected with Houston.

Many lament the ill feelings our citizens have toward our

democracy, and the Texas power-grab shows that a lot of cynicism originates from the top down and not the other way. All over the U.S., close neighbors could share a similar political perspective but their representation in their state legislature and U.S. Congress might be different. One neighbor may have voted for their victorious representative while the other a few blocks down in another district may have voted for a losing candidate. Effectively, one neighbor has representation and one does not. One is included as a political constituent while the other is excluded as a result of the bad luck of living on the wrong side of town.

Redistricting schemes benefit whomever called the shots at the time. Many are usually resolved between the parties in court. But those on the short end of the stick in 2001 will wait helplessly until the next redistricting in 2011, hoping the tide will turn in their favor. Until then, voters in legislative races are stuck as certain winners or losers in round after round of meaningless elections.

Incumbent lawmakers, by virtue of winner-take-all elections and designer districts, enjoy the ultimate advantage of a built-in super-majority. This is why so many run unopposed. Why would a challenger waste time and money running when the race is weighted so heavily in favor of the incumbent? Many incumbents go down due to criminal indictments or death before they lose their reelections. The basic rules of economics work with democracy too. Competition provides incentive for people to participate. Why have a Get Out The Vote drive in an uncontested election? Why even vote? Be it a 5% or 75% turnout, the result is the same—only one seat allocated in the legislature. Some of these lopsided districts draw third-party challengers, and Independents can benefit from the opening left by a sad, perennial major-party candidate who finally decides to call it quits after being unable to overcome the tall odds against him or her. But this is an exception to the spoiler rule, because for the most part only one party has any real chance to win.

Bipolar Disorder

OUR DEMOCRACY SWINGS from wasted votes to surplus votes in legislative races. At a certain point, a vote loses its value because of winner-take-all. Any vote over the threshold for election that a candidate receives is surplus; in a two-way race, any votes over 50% are unnecessary to win. If uncontested races dampen turnout, so do surplus votes. Why vote if you know your favorite legislative candidate is leading the race by a comfortable margin? A potential voter might be content in a designer district drawn to fit her political sensibilities; knowing her candidate was fitted for that district, the voter could stay home at ease. If a political-interest organization has the election in the bag for that district, why work for a greater turnout? Competitive top-of-the-ticket races like president or governor generally drive voter turnout. Yet the increased participation makes no impact whatsoever in uncontested legislative races.

Negative Promotions

COMPETITION TAKES A SADISTIC TURN in the political life-and-death battles of winner-take-all democracy; we either have a lopsided election where there's no incentive to learn about the issues and get involved, or we have a close election where the candidates each do their utmost to get voters to dislike their opponent. And contestants for election not only game opponents, voters are caught in their sights as well. Attack ads saturate the airwaves in the weeks leading up to an election. Campaign consultants, like skilled sharp-shooters, pick off voters and leave them out to dry. The noble discourse of the common folk in Norman Rockwell's America has given way to a form of electoral stalking.

I was in Minnesota in 2002 and happened to catch a creepy political ad on TV. It featured the eyes of a candidate moving from left to right with the zoom so tight that the image took up the whole screen. An ominous voice alleged the candidate's corruption while the close-up, grainy image of shifting eyes looped over and over. A fair conclusion would be that eyes moving are normal and part of how our bodies behave. But this is political cinema, and the hyper-zoom a trick of the camera used to discredit an opponent as a shifty crook. An insignificant nuance is amplified to full-blown character assassination.

Political attack ads are made to turn off voters. Winner-take-all elections are a zero-sum game. The rule is to turn away the people inclined to vote for an opponent. Those voters don't need to switch for the attacker; they can stay home, or head for the political wilderness. There need be only three voters left on election day: the two candidates and one person to choose between the lesser of two evils.

Primary Problems

VOTERS HAVE TO ENDURE the problems with our elections twice a year due to primary elections. Primaries share most of the problems with our general elections, and have additional obstacles all their own. They are a quasi-private/public affair. Parties are considered private organizations, but public monies pay for their internal functions. Voters need to declare an affiliation in a primary so that the free-association rights of a political party are preserved. The logic is that non-members cannot associate with private organizations. Parties could preserve their rights with nominating conventions or caucuses; some states do this with presidential races, but as far as congressional and legislative races go, public money pays for the nominating of private-party candidates to qualify for the general election. The real *free association* or *free ride* is Democrats, Republicans, and other qualifying parties using taxpayer funds to pay for their internal functions! Most primaries are redundant, because the majority of these races are uncontested. And because they lack competition, most are also poorly attended. Regardless of attendance, however, the cost to taxpayers is the same.

The notion of a secret ballot is one of the fundamentals of international election standards. But voters requesting an affiliated party ballot in a primary are blowing their privacy. The geographic lottery of redistricting adds insult to injury with primary elections; voters who find themselves on the losing side of gerrymandering not only lack representation in their government, they also have to pay for the internal functions of the private organizations responsible for disenfranchising them!

And because so many voters decline to participate, primary elections often produce candidates who don't necessarily reflect mainstream sensibilities. A mobilized minority can gain an influence disproportionate to their numbers by advancing their candidate to the general election from the small pool of primary voters. In a safe-seat district, the primary actually determines the election; this year, the Republican primary winner seeking an open seat in Newt Gingrich's old district in Georgia won't even face a token

Democrat in November. Taxpayers aren't the only ones spending money on two elections. Candidates for office must effectively run two campaigns. A tightly contested primary race can also be expensive, thus exacerbating the influence of special-interest money.

There is a growing movement toward qualifying primaries. With these, the top two vote-getters advance to the general election regardless of party affiliation. While this means more choices and privacy in the primary, in the general there will only be two candidates on the ballot. In the few competitive legislative races, third parties and Independents will not appear on the ballot. In many safe seats, as previously mentioned, incumbents will only be challenged by a token third party because the major on the losing side of gerrymandering won't bother to run. Things get even more distorted with a large field of candidates, because a person receiving just 15% or less of the vote in the primary can advance to the top two. Thus, candidates who lack mainstream support can nonetheless advance as a result of moderate candidates splitting a constituency.

The $3.9 Billion Democracy

REGARDLESS OF PRIMARY and general elections, American democracy has been tripping itself up for too long. It's remarkable that the same problems reoccur so often, but any mention of real reform is rarely heard. Millions of votes have been lost in our big elections for years, until our democracy experienced a virtual meltdown in the 2000 presidential election—then, of course, there were calls for reform. A commission was assembled with former Presidents Ford and Carter serving as co-chairs. Public hearings were held around the nation, with many recommendations put forth. The commission ultimately recommended sensible changes like preventing states from disenfranchising former felons, making election day a holiday, and closing polls in the presidential race at the same time.

On the heels of the commission's findings, Congress passed the Help America Vote Act of 2002 (HAVA). With HAVA, the federal government pledged $3.9 billion for states to upgrade old lever and punch-card voting machines. HAVA mandates every polling site to have at least one Direct Recording Electronic voting machine (DRE). DREs were intended to be a technological solution to our rickety election infrastructure. The course of our nation would no longer hang on a minute piece of perforated paper infamously known as a "chad." But in a gross oversight, HAVA never stipulated that DREs produce a paper record or utilize Open Source software. A voter will tap on an electronic screen to the tune of votes vanishing into the binaural void. Verification and recounts will be a matter of faith in pro-gramming. And because the technology's source code is proprietary, the public can't see what makes these rigs tick, so DREs also lack transparency. Too many voters lost faith as a result of the 2000 election debacle, and now they're expected to find comfort in a flawed technology. Touch-screen voting devices promised to take us over the bridge to a 21st-century trustworthy democracy. But some voters are already so suspicious that they refuse to vote on DREs—to the point where earlier this year the California Secretary of State went so far as to decertify all DREs used in their elections.

People are skeptical for good reason. This ill mood goes way beyond the shenanigans of the Florida recounts. HAVA backers never considered gerrymandering, wasted and surplus votes, or innovations to discourage negative campaign ads. They never considered obvious solutions, such as voting by mail with postage-paid return envelopes. Most importantly, paper mail ballots provide a voter-verifiable audit trail. In Washington State, 71% vote by mail. In Oregon, *all* elections are done by mail. $3.9 billion bought the appearance of progress, but among other lingering problems, too many voters still have to pay a governmental agency 37¢ to mail in their ballots.

What Is the Matter?

WHEN PEOPLE TELL ME they feel like their votes don't count, more than likely they are right as far as legislative races go. We need to make our democracy matter more to people. We can and should work to remedy the current situation. Anything less would be a resignation to stagnation and cynicism. Even worse, it would be admitting that the promise of democracy is just another shtick for tyrants to hide behind.

Chapter 4: Alternative Politics

THIS BEING THE U.S.A., there are always opportunities to move things forward. I am actually very enthusiastic about American democracy and the possibilities for real change. It's just a matter of getting the word out. Let's start to think about tangible solutions to fix our broken elections. Innovative reforms are in fact taking root in our nation.

Open-Source Democracy

THE POPULARITY OF THE INTERNET has grown immensely over the last ten years. While participation is down in elections, democracy is finding new life within the interaction of the web. People are connecting with new communication tools. Citizens discuss issues via message boards, or they physically come together in the form of "Meetups" (Meetup.com is a website that coordinates gatherings in cities around the world). The Internet has changed the communication paradigm 180 degrees. Candidates can't just push themselves on the electorate anymore; they need to pull voters in from online too. The Meetup phenomenon made its initial splash during Howard Dean's presidential campaign. I found it interesting that Dean supporters were gathering independently of the Democratic Party. This could be looked at as the makings of a de facto third party, or a third party waiting to be born under new electoral rules. Essentially, Dean was pulling in people while the Democratic Party was not.

The new wave of participation is also evident in the rise of the political weblogs, or blogs. The Internet is a wide-open space where the independently minded can flourish, and freed from the centralized, one-way flow of information, bloggers may have equal standing with the traditional media. For better or worse, the dialogue is open to anyone. Meetups and political blogs are part of a new "open-source" democracy. With Dean, decentralized like-minded voters found each other—on their own—to support a candidate who lacked the blessing of the establishment. Virtual communities transformed into real grassroots gatherings.

This is technology serving democracy in a meaningful way. Billions of federal dollars didn't create this open-source democracy; websites like Meetup.com are an example of innovations rooted in the competition of free enterprise. It will nonetheless be difficult for our uncompetitive legislative elections and distorted presidential campaigns to accommodate this vital new phenomenon. All of the barriers to participation will slow the movement down. The inequity of safe-seat incumbents enjoying a super-majority advantage, along with wasted and surplus votes, will pile up, obscuring the new promise of inclusion. Round after round of predictable elections will mean politics as usual.

IRV: Instant Runoff Voting

INSTANT RUNOFF VOTING, or IRV, can accommodate more choices in elections and promises to be popular simply because it saves voters' time—and taxpayers' money—by folding the function of a qualifying primary election into the general. IRV also protects privacy because there is no primary to declare affiliation.

With IRV, you vote for candidates in order of preference. In a field of four candidates, for example, you mark the ballot with a first choice, second choice, third choice, and fourth choice. As with any ballot, you can also choose not to vote for a candidate or candidates. If a candidate wins the majority of first choices, the election is over. If not, the instant runoff goes into effect and determines the majority winner. In a nutshell, the candidate wins who has the best balance of strong first-choice support *and* strong support as a second and possibly third choice. IRV remedies the problem of spoiler candidates and wasted votes. A constituent is free to vote his or her conscience and not worry about pre-election polls. She could vote for a third party, Independent, or outspoken major-party candidate as a first choice, and put a more cautious major-party candidate as second. People wouldn't feel compelled to picket Ralph Nader appearances anymore.

IRV not only accommodates electoral coalitions, it actually encourages them. Third parties could come in from the wilderness. People would be less cynical because they'd feel like their vote counted. Candidates would be more careful about engaging in negative advertising because they would want second-choice support too. Moderate candidates would tread lightly on the politically fruitful territory of the centrist voter. If IRV does benefit any kind of candidate, moderates tend to collect second- and third-choice support from the ideological margins of their respective constituencies. Some people ask if this method violates the principle of "one person, one vote," but it doesn't—every voter has one vote in each round of counting, just as in our current system. Primary elections, in fact, are already a process of winnowing candidates. I've voted for a different candidate in the primary than in the general election; that was effectively two votes, or choices, in the same election. IRV also makes campaigns less expensive because a candidate doesn't have to run two campaigns.

IRV folds a qualifying primary into the general election. It eliminates the lowest vote-getters, regardless of party affiliation, and distributes those choices until a majority winner is tabulated. Like other winner-take-all elections, it has a drawback. Due to the particular tabulation method, in a three-way race that requires an instant runoff, the candidate with the most second choices could be eliminated. Even so, IRV has more benefits for voters than stand-alone, exclusive primaries. It saves time and money, preserves privacy while protecting the free-association rights of parties. And most importantly, IRV gives voters more *real* choices.

The city of London and the country of Australia use IRV. San Francisco municipal elections will be held using IRV in fall 2004. Berkley, California and Vancouver, Washington have voted to start using it too. Utah Republicans now choose their statewide and congressional nominees with IRV. Some two-dozen colleges have adopted IRV, including Rice, Duke, the University of Massachusetts, and the University of Minnesota. The student vote to adopt it at Minnesota was a 76% yes majority.

People can be cautious about change, regardless of how much sense it makes. But once people become comfortable with IRV on a local level, it'll be an easy consideration for state and federal races, particularly when there's widespread perception in a given state that a key race was only won because of a spoiler. Instant Runoff Voting is an innovation that will reduce the barriers inhibiting participation, and could play a major role in reigniting democracy in the U.S.

Full Representation

OTHER NATIONS ENJOY voter turnout of up to 90%. We can take their best elements and build an electoral system that suits our own needs and values. Most modern democracies use full representation, also called proportional representation. Full representation and the lively, engaging, community-building politics it produces helps explain the high voter turnout in other countries. Some will say cultural differences between the U.S. and the rest of the world are why we have such low voter turnout. But that's like saying Americans are just a slovenly bunch of overweight couch potatoes too lazy to get down to the polls.

Full representation could remedy the discouraging situations we voters endure. As a reform, it goes beyond hanging chads or touch-screen machines. It is a fundamental reform that is modern and smart. Full representation is just like its title suggests. If a political party—or a cohesive group of independent-minded voters—earns 50% of the votes, it should earn 50% of the seats. If it earns 10% of votes, it should earn 10% of seats. Instead of single-member, winner-take-all districts, representation is allocated proportional to votes. Multi-member delegations are elected to their legislatures from geographically larger Super-Districts. Super-Districts can take down the walls against choice erected by winner-take-all, single-member districts, electing instead representative multi-member delegations to their legislatures.

Many people make the mistake of confusing the parliamentary systems that some countries in Europe use with full representation. In fact, this is the most common misperception I hear in discussions about electoral reform. I am not advocating we change our system of government. I only propose changing our system of elections. My plan is modest. I am advocating that we start by changing elections for our respective state houses only. If we're going to have both a state Senate and a state House, let's not elect them exactly the same way. Let's have one represent the areas of a state through small districts, and the other the people of the state through full-representation Super-Districts. Once it gains hold, full representation could usher in a new paradigm of vitality to stir up the epicenter of our political stasis—namely our capital, Washington, D.C.

Every state has its own issues and circumstances that can be accommodated with full representation. We citizens can build a modern democracy as we see fit. If we make sure that it is rooted in fairness, promotes inclusion, and is driven by the force of competition, we will be well on our way to a proportional system.

Here is my suggestion for a full-representation plan tailored for the state of Washington. Instead of forty-nine State House districts, I propose we create nine larger multi-member districts. Current U.S. House of Representatives boundary lines could make up the Super-Districts. Each district would elect eleven members to the State House. That would only increase the House membership from ninety-eight to ninety-nine. Political parties, or other groups of independent-minded voters, would run up to eleven candidates each on open party list ballots, with those candidates reflecting the full range of views and interests within that party. Voters would choose their favorite candidate from their favorite party. If a party wins 60%, their top six vote-getters go to the legislature. Even if a party receives only 10%, one candidate will be elected.

With Super-Districts, 90% of the voters will feel that they have representation. This will obviously make voting much more meaningful to millions of people. There will be no "safe seats" to give away to the incumbent parties. EVERY seat in a full-representation State House will be competitive. Political parties will stand in the marketplace of ideas *earning* their seats. Super-Districts make most voters winners, and could be the start of restoring confidence in our democracy. Every Republican and Democratic voter will have representation in their State House. They will hold the real value of being an actual constituent. Democracy will not be over on the first Wednesday of November—that's when too many voters fall into the moribund "loser" columns of election returns. No longer will voters have to hold their breath until the next round of decennial redistricting, hoping they fall on the winning side of a geographic lottery. A full-representation State House will finally carry the moniker of the "People's House" authentically. Inclusion will be the rule that invites participation. We can make sure major parties are truly accountable by opening up our elections to third parties, and voters will finally have real choices. Competition for voters will create the incentive for parties to cultivate new constituencies. Wasted and surplus votes will be minimized. "Wasted voters" will be led back in from the wilderness with the promise and dignity of having actual representation in the People's House.

Party Lists

A PARTY LIST is a roster of candidates published by each political organization. A good party list should reflect a diverse array of citizens, and a team of eleven party members could canvass a whole district in a system of Super-Districts. They could attend events all together, in smaller groups, or individually. At the same time, they'd not only be competing against rival parties, they would work to be the top vote-getters of their respective party. I believe that's a healthy incentive for candidates to be the best campaigners they can.

Of course, money makes an impact all its own. A self-financed candidate has an advantage regardless of what electoral system is used. (It's been said that in politics, money is like water—it finds a way.) But given a wide range of choices, most voters will support someone based on really believing they are the best candidate for them—and that belief is hard to buy when voters have real choices with a range of views. Year after year, the lack of participation of our youth in elections is lamented. But a party could have candidates that look, talk, and care about issues affecting young people by actually *having* young people on their list. Imagine the potential for young people to reconnect with our democracy!

Getting elected is no simple matter, and seats are not just up for grabs with Super-Districts. A frequent criticism of full-representational systems is the possible fragmentation of the governing body. This is a reasonable concern. A tenuous fragmentation could be an issue if we were considering electing all the State House members at-large. With ninety-eight members, that would mean the threshold for representation would be around 1%. Indeed, so-called fringe groups and people with irrational perspectives could more easily get elected. (They do under the current system anyway . . .)

Germany remedied electoral fragmentation years ago by imposing a 5% threshold—for the sake of political stability, a party or candidate must cross the 5% line to win. With Super-Districts, a party or candidate would need almost twice that threshold, or 9% of the vote, to merit election. It's typical for around 300,000 voters to turn out in a U.S. congressional election. That means it would take about 27,000 votes to win a single seat. 27,000 is about the same number of votes candidates currently need to gain a seat in the Washington State House. So, in effect, the bar is neither lowered nor raised—though dialogue and debate in the legislature would now include the viewpoints of a much higher percentage of the population.

Third parties will need to appeal to the majority mainstream sensibilities of Washington voters to win. Fringe candidates will likely stay on the sidelines, unable to cross the high threshold built into Super-Districts. Ultimately, if a party offers an unappealing message with weak candidates, they will not win anything—but that's their problem. Increased competition will drive Get Out The Vote efforts. Surplus votes will never exceed 9%. If a political organization conducting a GOTV drive finds its efforts gaining by 7%, they'll be compelled to push harder for the 2% of voters to cross the threshold and win another seat for their cause. That means more work, more engagement with folks, and more vitality for our elections. Competing parties would work the whole district. Urban *and* rural issues would be spoken to in the race for more seats.

There will not only be competition for voters in this scenario, the real opportunities created could drive a dynamic inside of the respective parties. Intra-party competition could start at a privately funded and organized caucus. The 2004 Washington Democratic presidential caucuses were fueled by the force of competition, since these caucuses are not subject to a winner-take-all system. Precinct meetings bulged to overflow capacity with citizens who wanted a say in who got to run for president. The Republican caucuses, on the other hand, were a mere matter of procedure—as their candidate, George W. Bush, was an incumbent—with a handful of party members in each precinct going through the motions of nominating their candidate. (This is another example of competition driving turnout.)

I attended my precinct caucus as a Democrat who wanted a voice in nominating our candidate for president. It was a small rural meeting, but nonetheless a model of political discourse. We debated the merits of our candidates in a respectful, straightforward manner. We were charting the course of where we thought our nation should go by utilizing the democratic devices afforded us. Anybody who declared an affiliation to our party was included in the discussion. We were engaging in civic affairs while protecting the free-association rights of our organization. After the back and forth we voted on our nominee. Bad feelings were negated because we were using a proportional system that represented people well and, as with IRV, gave people a chance to support their second choice if their first choice lacked favor.

Just imagine if the Democrats had used our antiquated winner-take-all system for their nominating process. With the old system, the Democratic primary would have been over by the time our state's turn came around. Our caucus would have had a meager turnout similar to the Republicans. John Kerry would have taken all the surplus votes in the earlier contests for himself, crossing the threshold for nomination. The other candidates would not have won *any* delegates, regardless of respectable second- or third-place showings. The positive attributes of the proportional, or full-representation system were quite evident. While Kerry was the ultimate winner, all of the other challengers will have delegates at their respective state and national conventions. The Democrats will benefit from the proportional system because of its inherent inclusiveness. Party unity is served because contention is minimized. People feel better about the process because there is more equity. With Super-Districts, a party caucus could take place every two years, as party members would assemble for the task of nominating the eleven members for the open-list ballot. Unlike with partisan primaries, public monies would not be used for these private functions.

Whatever means a party uses to come up with its list is the private affair of the organization. A group of, say, five independent-minded people could join together to run and hope for just one name to get elected. They'd need to come up with a name and comply with ballot access rules. If they had good exposure, a comprehensive message, and drew enough votes, they could send their top vote-getter to the legislature. There is an incentive for all members on the list to work hard; the winning candidate could take a couple of their list-mates to work as paid staff in the House.

A Higher Body

PEOPLE CRITICIZE PARLIAMENTARY democracies as being unstable. In a parliamentary system, the majority coalition is the ruling government. If it fractures, the coalition loses its majority and the government collapses. Our bicameral system, with the added check of an executive officer (the governor), provides greater stability. Super-Districts would not alter the election of state senators. I propose my state's forty-nine senatorial districts remain unchanged. Currently, the only major difference between the State House and Senate is the number of members and length of their terms. State senators serve four-year terms and only half the Senate is up for election in a given year, ensuring continuity in government; thus the Senate is referred to as a "higher body." This provides a counterweight to the two-year terms for members of the full-representation People's House. The idea for these shorter terms is to have a responsive government. Again, why have two chambers that are elected the same way?

The notion of minority rule is the biggest bogeyman conjured by people who misunderstand proportional systems. It can be said that our current system already promotes minority rule. A single chair of a legislative committee can simply refuse to hear a bill before them—that's how much power a chairmanship wields. Another example is our discouragingly low election turnouts. If turnout in 2002 was 40%, that means the ruling party in the U.S. House was elected by around 20% of the voters! I won't mention the people who don't even bother to register, let alone vote. And a good many of the people who did vote didn't actually elect a candidate; they fell in the loser column on election night. How's that for minority rule? A well-designed proportional system will minimize the problem—and that's the point. For we can make the best electoral process however we want.

Chapter 5:
Let's Fix This Broken Democracy!

THE POLICTICAL SYSTEM in the U.S.A. is long overdue for reform. Things are not moving. This is the kind of condition where a spark for change can ignite. I've seen the music world turned around from an inside perspective: The genesis of the change in 1991 came from individuals who refused to accept the status quo and made their own way. Music and politics are similar because they are both about people coming together. There is a hunger for change.

I offer these electoral reforms for people to wrap their minds around. We need to determine if such methods best meet our nation's needs and values, as well as remedy the reduction in electoral participation by the citizenry. We don't need to change our U.S. Constitution to implement the ideas I'm proposing.

My goal is to get people to start thinking outside the box. A real discussion about these reforms has yet to start. I'd like to see more states do what British Columbia, my Canadian neighbor to the north, is doing. The government has sponsored a year-long process where a citizens group representing the whole province is debating a new electoral system. Its choice will then be presented to the voters. Deliberation and communication—what a great idea! The media laments our widespread disconnection with our government, but where are the ideas to move us forward? Newspapers and television programs fill miles of print and countless hours reporting on the abuses our democracy endures, but meaningful electoral reforms are barely on the radar.

Election reform advocate Steven Hill likens a voting method to a computer operating software. The hardware of our three branches of government is fine; it's our operating system that is outdated. It's like we're stuck in the early DOS programs while our processors are capable of handling much more sophisticated technology. Our Constitution has evolved over the course of the last two and a quarter centuries, while our election systems have remained the same. It's like we've crossed the bridge to the 21st century in an 18th-century horse and buggy.

It's going to be a hard road toward the reforms I'm advocating. Simple fear of change prevents many new ideas from being implemented. Put this alongside the agendas of those who benefit from the current arrangement and you've got the formula for stasis. Washington and Iowa are moving in the right direction; both states have commissions that draw district boundaries. In Washington, our commission has a mandate to make districts competitive. Many are, and as a result voter participation is higher than the national average. Some seats are still considered "safe" due to the difficulty in creating competitive boundaries in certain areas; this is one reason why a third of Washington's legislative races were uncontested in 2002. In that same year, turnout was only about half of registered voters. I believe that commissions are a good start toward resolving the appalling conflict of interest legislators exhibit when charged with their own redistricting.

United We Stand

AGAIN, THIS IS THE UNITED STATES, and there are many opportunities within our two-party system to make meaningful progress. The halls of the legislature are open by design. It's hard to make it to many hearings in state capitols that can be far away, especially during the working week, but there are plenty of organizations that have a good grasp of what's going on in legislative sessions. These groups are always looking for more help with their efforts. Many municipalities hold public hearings in the evening for the convenience of working people. And we must not forget that local politics are an important component to our democracy. Currently there are numerous elections to participate in. School levies and other publicly financed endeavors are always up for a vote. Some states have an initiative process. Ballot measures are easy, for they require a simple yes or no vote. (IRV and full representation can also serve our local governments.)

People grumble about the two major parties, but they throw out the baby with the bath water when they disparage political parties in general. I believe the key to successful advocacy is to band together with like-minded folks. That's what the essence of a political party is—the convergence of people who share the same sensibilities and needs. When people get together in a significant way, the powers-that-be take notice.

One need not start his or her own party. The current situation can already accommodate motivated people. Most of our democratic institutions are suffering from a lack of participation. This starts with the two major parties themselves. Chances are, your local precinct is lacking in membership. This creates opportunities to move up into leadership positions fairly quickly. In places with more robust activity, a person could at least head up a committee on an issue near and dear to her heart. Membership in civic organizations has been declining for years too. There is a famous Diane Arbus photo of men wearing fezzes riding around in little cars in a Main Street parade. The image is symbolic of the perception of institutions of civic participation being an anachronism to the point of being surreal. Such institutions have never recovered from the generation gap of the 1960s. Since then, many youth have taken their messages to the streets in the form of protesting. Perhaps the old institutions were slow to change or too timid to question the establishment? Regardless, their membership has been dropping parallel to the death rates of the pre–baby boomers.

People like the fun of a good show regardless. During the WTO protests, downtown Seattle brimmed with protesters clad in post-modern garb expressing themselves in a manner not much different from what those buggy-driving Shriners were doing—I witnessed a few people sporting fezzes too! People scream about the virtual integration of corporate special interests with our government but ignore the epidemic of lack of civic participation. Politics abhors a vacuum. Too many are wandering the political wilderness angry, unable to see the way out of the woods. I can only imagine if all of the positive energy and creativity of the WTO protests were channeled into conventional politics—and if we had an electoral system that would allow ongoing connections between those applying street heat and those seeking change from within. (I wonder how many protesters have run for elected office in a major-party primary since the '99 WTO . . .) People of all ages, from all walks of life, are concerned about the course of our nation. This reality transcends any notion of "cutting edge" or hip. Why can't the local Elks lodge host a Bhutto performance on the inequities of globalization? How about a poetry slam at the Eagles Hall about media consolidation?

Many civic institutions are places where issues are discussed within a democratic forum. Resolutions are passed. Officers are elected from the ranks of membership. If the "fraternal" group is nonpartisan, all the better for the notion of inclusion. Like the major parties on the local level, the vitality of many of these organizations peaked years ago and their membership is in decline. But they have the infrastructure, through years of existence, for the civic-minded to get off to a running start. There are buildings with kitchens, auditoriums with stages, and even full bars, yet these venues sit idle or are sparsely attended—even though their name carries weight in a community and with lawmakers. There are so many Moose, Eagle, Elk, Grange, and Shriner organizations, among others, that could use an influx of new energy. With so many to choose from, there's got to be *one* that could fit a person's sensibilities. That's why there are, or were, so many of them in the first place.

I am a member of my local Grange. The Grange is a rural activist organization that was founded soon after the Civil

War. Where I live, it acts as the city or community hall. It is a venue for people to come together for the common good. If we do need to reinvent the wheel, let's create new civic organizations along the democratic lines of the old ones. In the U.S., we have a standard of living that affords us the opportunity to actually enjoy ourselves while still keeping a civic consciousness. Let's work to preserve, and maybe rescue, our way of life while creating and maintaining real human connections.

Inclusion Must Always Win

AS OUR HISTORY SHOWS, American democracy does make progress. In the course of our great experiment, the U.S.A. has had its share of challenges. 2001 marked the thirty-year anniversary of the ratification of the 26th Amendment to the Constitution, which lowered the voting age to eighteen. There was a war raging in Southeast Asia, yet the idea of democracy had a chance to evolve to include young people. In 1965, during the early years of that same painful conflict, the Voting Rights Act was signed into law, making democracy more inclusive toward African-Americans and others who had been shut out because of prejudice. And it was in 1920 that women finally won their right to vote. All of these events are looked back on with pride, because they demonstrate the evolution of a democracy toward greater and greater inclusion. Every time the franchise has been expanded, legislators elected under the old rules supported the change. We shouldn't let people tell us that reforms can't be won.

As I've mentioned, third-party and Independent voters and candidates are not the only ones excluded from our two-party system. Low participation reveals that most of our citizens are not finding meaning in our democracy. The cycle of reinvention, in the context of the human experience, can be seen as a search for meaning. People look for meaning in popular music, which goes through trends that operate in a cycle. Once music becomes predictable, and a formula to sustain the establishment, people become cynical, stop buying the music, and tune out. But this sad state of affairs opens the gates for the new wave of bands. The new sounds draw people back in, thus restoring vitality.

People also look for meaning in democracy. Once democracy becomes predictable, and a formula to sustain the establishment, people become cynical, stop voting, and tune out. It is now time for a new wave in civic consciousness in our nation. Innovative reforms like Instant Runoff Voting and full representation are taking root. They are proven, and they work.

As I have said, there is an inherent resistance to change. But change comes for better or worse so let's make sure we're progressing. Democracy is not an absolutist dogma. It's

merely a forum that accommodates good ideas and redundant arguments alike. I offer these reforms to you, kind reader,
as food for thought. My thoughts are on a method to rein-
vigorate our civic consciousness. Many are cynical and dis-
connected. People feel like our democracy isn't moving. It's
like a bad relationship, where people feel stuck. We *should*
be angry and frustrated. (If this is starting to sound like a
self-help book, so be it.) It's okay to feel that way, because
we're getting prodded by greater forces. Only we, as a
nation, can fix the situation. We can't do it alone. How can
somebody advocate democracy with virtually nobody knowing about their work?

Cynicism toward elected officials is universal, but why do
other democracies enjoy much higher voter turnouts? We
consider our nation the world's greatest democracy, yet
expecting the high turnout enjoyed by other nations is dis-
missed as naïve. Why not strive for these numbers? Too
many have resigned in sheer discouragement. This need not
be so. Let us look to our fundamentals of freedom, inclusion,
and fairness. If we wrap these principles with innovation, we
can continue down the path our founders embarked on
some 228 years ago.

For more information, visit the website of the Center for Voting and Democracy, fairvote.org, or Krist Novoselic's electoral-reform website, fixour.us.

KRIST NOVOSELIC was born in Compton, California in 1965 and grew up in Croatia and Aberdeen, Washington. He was a founding member of the legendary rock band Nirvana, and along with bandmates Kurt Cobain and David Grohl, Novoselic helped to change the course of music history in 1992 when Nirvana snapped up *Billboard* magazine's number one spot with their highly acclaimed album, *Nevermind*, which went on to sell millions of copies around the world. Nirvana opened the doors for a new generation of musicians and bands. After Nirvana, Novoselic went on to become one of rock music's most politically minded musicians. He has committed himself to numerous community projects and is now an influential political voice in Washington State. *Of Grunge and Government* is Krist Novoselic's first book, and he currently lives in Southwest Washington State.